OVERCOMMUNICATION
OVERCOMMUNICATION
OVERCOMMUNICATION
OVERCOMMUNICATION
OVERCOMMUNICATION
OVERCOMMUNICATION
OVERCOMMUNICATION
OVERCOMMUNICATION
OVERCOMMUNICATION
OVERCOMMUNICATION
OVERCOMMUNICATION

RESIST PHONY ENCORES!

GRUFF RHYS

For all my signs

Art direction and design: Mark James

PLEASE DON'T.

That's just the name of my first band, translated.

We were called...

FFA COFFI PAWB

It means 'everybody's coffee beans'.

As there are no taboo words in the Welsh language, or most languages for that matter, we have to borrow swear words from English for shock value. Ffa coffi sounds very much like fuck off. 'I pawb' means 'to everybody' or, simply put: 'fuck off, everyone'. It's a play on words particularly attractive to a teenager.

I formed the band with my friend Rhodri Puw when we were 16.

I left school around the same time. It was 1986.

All Ffa Coffi Pawb songs were in Welsh, my first language. But the chorus to the 1988 song 'Valium', I suppose, is in English. Another play on words. I love that space in-between languages, but this book is about the spaces between songs.

FFA COFFI PAWB

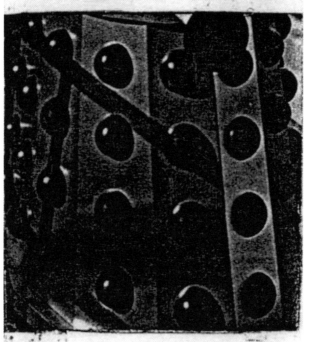

valium

VALIUM
VALIUM
VALIUM
VALI(Y)UM
YUM.YUM

At 17 I moved from the mountains to the closest city, Bangor, and lived in a shared house. The song ('Valium') deals with a house-mate, who was recently discharged from the army due to his schizophrenia. He used to chase me and threaten to kill me with an axe when he wasn't on his medication, Valium. (Valium was a precursor of Diazepam, a quaint, light prescription drug when compared to today's heavy prescribed opiates.)

I used to lock myself in the bathroom, much as Shelley Duvall did in Stanley Kubrick's 'The Shining'.

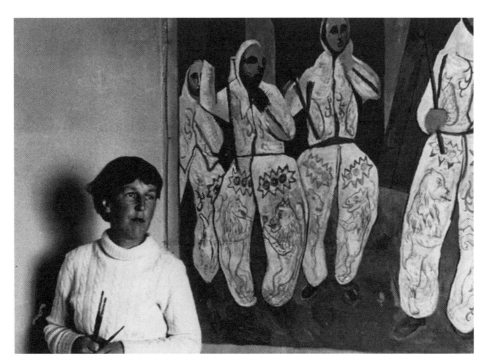

It was a large three-storey house turned into bedsits and flats. Some years earlier, one of my favourite authors*, the artist Brenda Chamberlain, had died in the same house from an overdose of barbiturates.

In the 1930s she was the area's first hippie. When I grew up, old women had tales of her wearing nothing but a flour sack, with holes cut out for her head and arms.

A middle-aged ex-sailor lived in a basement bedsit. One day I returned to find a smoking bonfire in front of the house. Some kids had broken in and taken lots of his belongings outside and set them alight. I passed him in the corridor a few hours later. He looked dazed and upset. "SOMEONE'S TAKEN ALL MY POSSESSIONS," he said, staring at his broken door. He eventually moved out. He was replaced by a blonde fellow who suffered from manic depression, as they used to call it. I eventually wrote a song called 'Slashed Wrists This Christmas' about his thankfully unsuccessful suicide attempt.

(* I recommend 'Tide-Race' and 'A Rope of Vines')

The 1980s were a very dark time for many people and I feel privileged to have had not only the care, comfort, and enthusiasm of my family as I threw myself headlong into a life of music that neither of us could fully comprehend, but also the support of a still just-about-functioning social security system that facilitated an independent life of music for me as a young person from the age of 16, when I wasn't working or in education. Social security and housing benefit for the under-18s were cut by Margaret Thatcher's government the year after I turned that corner. That fragility within society certainly set the tone for my songs in that period, and my outlook towards the frivolity of performance.

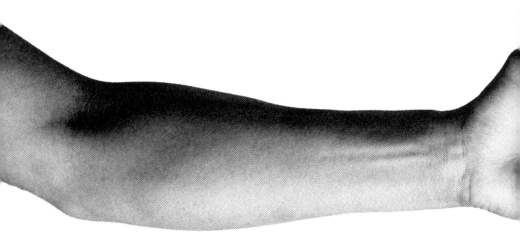

Ffa Coffi Pawb started to play live all over Wales and gradually we became quite popular within the Welsh-speaking community. Though mostly we seemed to play the Normal College's student union bar. This was a subsidised, low pressure, informal space where we could experiment.

At the start, we were inspired by some German industrial bands to use power tools in our live set for their piercing noise. Mostly I would drill into metal, or Rhodri's electric guitar whilst he played (it was his dad's drill after all). Through trial and thankfully no error, I discovered that I could create the illusion of drilling myself in the stomach if I wore a particular jumper of mine.

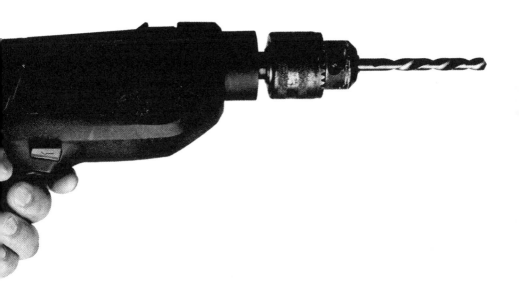

The drill bit, placed to appear as if I was about to drill into my belly button or thereabouts, would gather in the nylon-and-cotton-hybrid material of the sweater up to a point where it couldn't turn anymore and a safety shutdown function would kick in. Not only was it a cheap attention-seeking stage gag but it was also a highly effective strategy in alienating the squares from the pataphysical studies course in attendance. It seemed (to me at least) that I was genuinely drilling myself in the stomach.

In the late 1980s there were three colleges in the city of Bangor: the more vocational Gwynedd Technical College (where, after years of failure, at 19 I managed to complete an art course and left Bangor for the bright lights and communal dance-music of a Polytechnic in the big city); the University of Wales* for the studious; and the Normal College, which was more like a Polytechnic and where the more normal people attended.

Ffa Coffi Pawb's bass player Dewi Emlyn was three years older and attended the Normal College. It's where the Beatles, some of the Stones and Marianne Faithful came in '67 for a seminar run by the Indian guru Maharishi Mahesh Yogi.

A good place to hang out, I used to stay at Dewi's halls of residence occasionally if I'd missed the last bus home and if there was no spare bed I'd sleep in the interior phone booth where the Beatles had learned of their manager Brian Epstein's demise 20 years earlier.

And even though I wasn't sharing the same time as the Beatles, at least I was sharing the same space. When Lennon was shot I was 10 years old and as they re-screened the Beatles' movies over the subsequent days on TV, my love for melodic songwriting was cemented.

*or the 'University of Whales' as mentioned by John Lennon's character in the 'Yellow Submarine' movie

The Beatles and friends at the Normal College, 1967

In this stone-walled vestibule, where hundreds of other stressful and emotional phone calls had also likely taken place, as I slept I could practically smell the melodic residue of McCartney.

I started to travel beyond Wales to see other bands play live, bands that seemed to maintain that melodic tradition in some equally transcendent way, including Spacemen 3, My Bloody Valentine, and The Jesus and Mary Chain. None of these bands talked or communicated to the audience in any way. I found this to be very refreshing. They weren't condescending in the way that overly-charismatic bands with members who talked to the audience were. At the time I found commands from stage to be very patronising.

PUT YOUR HANDS IN THE AIR

It was a revelation for me, suddenly there was little pressure for me to communicate with the audience, when all I was interested in was writing and singing songs. Which was just as well as I had very little in the way of social skills, and couldn't speak very clearly or look an audience in the eye, and I wasn't interested in people having a good time.

Ffa Coffi Pawb split up after seven years, three studio albums, and almost no onstage banter. Except the odd home-made t-shirt with various comments written in ironed-on text transfers:

REV IS DEAD

(referring to a short-lived pop movement),

COCOEN

{lamb's penis} and so on.

After we split, I formed Super Furry Animals with Dafydd Ieuan, my Bangor flatmate, cosmic mentor, and Ffa Coffi Pawb drummer, his brother Cian, and our Cardiff friends Huw and Guto. We became quite popular and I found myself fronting a rock band that had gold discs. Audiences were large and I started to feel I should communicate general logistical information to them.

By our fourth show I had stolen the title of a 1960s piece by the conceptual artist Bruce Nauman as a directive of what the audience should do:

PAY ATT
MOTHER

ENTION
UCKERS

That seemed to work for a while, but in general the mumbling tone of my voice didn't successfully cut through the reverberant PAs of the pop industry. The 'festival wind'* phenomenon, which seems to blow sound around, didn't help.

For over a decade from 1995 I mumbled my way around the world, for the most part being misunderstood if I talked for too long. (When in-ear monitors were introduced, any onstage banter disappeared as we were mixed into separate audio cocoons.) Cavernous venues built for scale rather than acoustics meant that often I couldn't define what I was saying either. But I'd try and throw out a sentence into the cavern, like:

THANK YOU, THIS SONG IS CALLED SOMETHING OR OTHER

Sometimes there would be some kind of reaction, but for the most part not ...

I tried out many strategies in my quest to communicate clearly and bond with the audience. In 1996 we performed the song

GOD! SHOW ME MAGIC

at the Smash Hits Roadshow at Cardiff arena. I was coming up on MADOG — a fictional Welsh drug — dressed in a panda outfit screaming one of my own finely-crafted slogans ...

PROPERTY IS THEFT!

to thousands of screaming pop music fans,

PROPERTY IS THEFT!

Over and over again.

We shared the dressing room with Australian pop sensation Peter Andre. "Wow guys, I love your outfits, do you wear them for every show?" he marvelled politely and inquisitively at our array of over-sized animal and alien attire. We left as soon as possible, steering our Judo instructor's sister away from him as we made to leave.

"MAE O'N GORJYS," she screamed earnestly in the Welsh language as we all escaped together down the corridor. She was a teacher at a secondary school.

THE VAN

Sometimes the practicalities of performing involve
unexpected logistics, completely unbeknown to the
audience. In the year 1999, now into our fourth year of
touring relentlessly, we were given a late-night slot
at the Glastonbury Festival playing to tens of thousands
of people. It was to be screened live to a further few
million folk on TV. On paper it seemed like an award for
all those years of toil.

Shortly before starting the first song, however, a guy
backstage asked if we could delay our set as he wanted
to drive his van across the field. He seemed highly
agitated and was particularly delusional. Someone
explained that it would be better for him to wait until
after the show due to the large numbers of people on said
festival field.

Between songs I could hear him screaming at me from the side
of the stage to stop playing as he wanted to leave NOW! At a
certain point he could wait no longer and he started to
drive directly into the audience around 50 meters in front
of the stage. I had an excellent view. Various technicians
shouted at me to ask the audience to be careful and move
clear in case of fatalities, etc.

I watched in horror as he seemed to plough through the
audience. I had no training in how to command such a large
group of people to defuse the situation; surely there was
someone else in charge here? But all eyes were on me.
Theoretically a microphone and a large PA system gives
you an outsized voice, but nothing came out of my mouth. The
wonderful, spirited audience eventually engulfed the
dangerous moving van with sheer human volume. They used
it as a podium to dance on.

The agitated driver also climbed up on the roof and tried to wrestle the dancers to the ground. Eventually he succeeded, and finally realising he couldn't move the van along any further in the intense sea of people he decided to dance alone on top of the van (he was quite good and very expressive). It coincided with a song called 'The Man Don't Give a Fuck', which had an amazing extended techno breakdown by Cian Ciarán, perfect for dancing. The Van-come-podium was located in front of the stage in quite a geometrically-pleasing location. Members of Scottish post-rock band Mogwai joined us incognito on stage dressed in our alien outfits with their fists aloft.

Afterwards people thought it was some kind of publicity stunt by the band. It was a memorable experience that went way beyond musical transcendence into another indefinable chaotic realm. But maybe it's not always about the music or the artist for that matter. Maybe it's about the crowd.

As we refined our sound, thankfully the music and the video projections behind us became very powerful and I didn't need to communicate much more beyond singing the songs.

In 2004, I played a solo show on the same bill as the Argentinian artist Juana Molina. She used a sampler to loop her voice in the moment to hypnotic effect. And before long, apparently sheep-like in retrospect, I started to use a similar technique.

In 2005, I released a solo record called 'Yr Atal Genhedlaeth' featuring a track called 'Gwn Mi Wn' which means 'Yes, I Know', featuring vocal loops.

Sampling myself during solo shows meant there were extended passages when I could sit back and relax as the music looped with no further involvement from myself needed. I bought a small blackboard and began to write messages to the audience. At Super Furry Animals shows, meanwhile, visionary guitarist Huw Bunford and I started to create signs with taped lettering, card, and pens.

By 2008, whilst touring with the electro-pop group Neon Neon, I upgraded to fancy printed signs. Playing shows with super-articulate MCs and the lightning-rod charisma of American singers and rappers, like Har Mar Superstar, Spankrock, and Yo! Majesty, I discovered that I had no comparable energy. Deadpan was the only way for me to go. So, I started to employ TV-production-style cue cards.

We further expanded these messages and commands at SFA shows where either I or Bunf (pictured) would always suggest that the audience should RESIST PHONY ENCORES!

which is a core belief of the band. It was based on a poster I had once seen on an Irish tour in Derry:

RESIST BRITISH RULE

Whatever the deeply problematic pit-
falls of appropriating the language
of protest into the world of benign
entertainment, this poster inspired a
multitude of further signs. We had one
placard with

RESIST VONDA SHEPARD

written on it. Vonda was an MOR piano balladeer
who had written the theme song for a TV drama
concerning a Boston-based lawyer, Ally McBeal.
I was worried that she was the tip of a new MOR
iceberg of piano balladeers that would destroy
music, but I think I overreacted. There were much
bigger threats to our pop civilisation, and now
I feel like such a dick. It was the pinnacle of her
career perhaps. I raise a glass to her and the
pataphysical studies students at the Normal
College. I'm so sorry, what the fuck was I thinking?

Gradually I began to use—and refine the use of—the signs in all my shows. I was amazed at how easy it was to manipulate the audience when using direct commands. Audiences became, not putty in my hands, but co-conspirators elevating our collective spirits onto a higher plane. If only I could have come up with this stuff a decade earlier! The shift in audience behaviour was phenomenal!

I began to figure how a trajectory of cue cards, held aloft in the right order, could lift an audience in a very short space of time. It needed no energy or charismatic projection from myself beyond lifting the cards.

A sign bearing the word

APPLAUSE!

would bring polite applause. I would savour the moment briefly then turn the sign around.

On the back was printed

LOUDER!

The applause would grow and excitement levels increased accordingly. If I was feeling like it, I would then deploy a sign featuring:

APE
SHIT

The crowd would go predictably ape-shit.

These are quite simple, base commands with fairly predictable results. But to reach true riotous delirium, an emotional resonance is required. It's why populist politicians often seek to shift campaigns on to an emotional footing and away from policy detail.

This is where I began to notice discrepancies and regional variations in my audience. Using the terms of crowd psychology, my audience could be viewed as a

PSYCHO-
LOGICAL
GROUP

in that they had chosen to come to my show and therefore, arguably, were representative of a particular psychological shared sensibility, as opposed to a

PHYSICAL GROUP

of strangers randomly grouped together in a bus station, for example.

Just like fans of a particular football team, the psychological group are supporting the same side, wish their experience to be a good one, and are mostly susceptible to mild audience participation.

During a tour of the nations of Britain for my third solo album, 'Hotel Shampoo', I started to deploy a fourth sign into my 'frenzy medley'. Starting the tour in Wales, which has some of the most economically-fragile areas in Western Europe, a traditionally small private sector and comparatively very few rich people, holding up my fourth sign, the un-nuanced 'TAX THE RICH', connected emotionally in an instant to near riotous effect. As the tour advanced I found the sign to have a similar effect in the North of England and particularly in Scotland. The tour climaxed with a show at The Shepherd's Bush Empire in West London. The biggest venue of the tour where one could expect the loudest audience response. Taking down my Ape Shit sign and surveying a bubbling mass of hysteria in front of me, I turned the sign around and lifted the ultimate in uplifting signs:

What I hadn't considered was the demographic of my London audience. I was, by now an ageing 41-year-old indie rock musician. In the Socialist Republic of Wales, Scotland, and the regions of England, my gigs would be attended by an open-minded type of music fan; with an ear attuned to specialist radio, access to record reviews, enough money for the ticket, perhaps, but given the underfunding of public-sector wages and decimation of the former industrial heartlands, not likely to be particularly wealthy.

In London, however, in addition to the generic person above, there would also be an element of financially-successful, even rich, private-sector workers, living in the affluent bubble of what was at the time the wealthiest and most expensive city in Europe. I held the sign aloft. The atmosphere dropped from APE SHIT to a confused state, as some in the audience scrambled to make sense of this new directive. 'TAX THE RICH?' Whole chunks of the audience seemed to be stunned into a silent, uncomfortable panic.

Others jumped up and down in continued joy, but the audience were now just a physical group. The shared psychology was gone. We were random people placed together at a bus station where a portion were waiting for limousines. As the originator or shepherd of the frenzy, I had broken the spell.

A pioneer in the study of group psychology in the 19th century, Gustav Le Bon*, gave crowds a bad name. For him sovereign individuals acted in meaningful ways, while groups of people became violent mobs who behaved irrationally.

[*No relation to Cate Le Bon who is a great artist, pictured]

This is countered today by contemporary psychologists, such as Stephen Reicher*, who believes a member of a crowd is not necessarily a PAWN but an AGENT within a collective agency.

[*As an eminent representative in his field he was approached during the 2020 Covid-19 lockdown by the UK Government to advise their COBRA emergency meetings on the collective psychology of the British people, in the face of new and extreme self-quarantine directives. In turn he became a leading critic of the Government when their own members started to publicly break quarantine rules that were still adhered to by the general public, thus blunting the bond of trust between the leader and the crowd.]

ARE YOU A

PAWN

OR AN

GENT?

OR A

PAWN

RESEMBLING A

SECRET

AGENT?

By labelling gatherings as mobs, and scaring the public away from collectivism, Reicher argues that Le Bon was actually driving the public away from the only resource they could plausibly harness to change the dire unfair reality of late-19th-century life. The resource that is the powerful agency of an individual within the collectivism of a crowd.

Beyond my previous caricature, London can also be a very compassionate city of course. Here's a picture of the march against the 2003 war in Iraq which I attended. The protest was a warning to Tony Blair and George Bush that they were mistaken to believe that Iraq had so-called weapons of mass destruction. The protestors also believed that going to war in the manner these crazed leaders had in mind would destabilise the entire region for decades. Although people were protesting about more or less the same thing you can see from the placards that the various messages are nuanced and autonomous. These people, spanning a whole spectrum of political alignments, are agents of change acting collectively with no leader in sight.

Arguably, therefore, crowd problems only arise through bad leadership.

In the course of my research for this book I phoned Reicher from that same Bangor vestibule I used to sleep in as a teenager and where the Beatles heard of their manager's death. In a co-authored paper, he has stated

'THE DEVELOPMENT OF A SHARED SOCIAL IDENTITY IS THE BASIS OF INFLUENTIAL AND CREATIVE LEADERSHIP'

But he also states:

'AN IDENTITY THAT IS OUT OF KILTER WITH REALITY AND THAT HAS NO PROSPECT OF BEING REALIZED, ON THE OTHER HAND, WILL SOON BE DISCARDED IN FAVOUR OF MORE VIABLE ALTERNATIVES'

Here's a photo of the deposed, out-of-kilter Italian leader Mussolini in 1945. By 1946 Italy had voted by referendum to depose their royal family (blamed by many for helping to facilitate fascism) and became a republic.

Of course, a life of entertainment, the occasional wearing of panda outfits in public, and leading the masses with comedic cue cards are acts of buffoonery. Fleeting moments of levity, culturally interesting at best, but politically benign perhaps? But what if the buffoon entertainer becomes a political leader? The joke soon ceases to be funny. And as our planet rapidly collapses into post-populist buffoon isolationism or, if you prefer, POPOBUIS it feels like the joke is on us?

The language and behaviour of light entertainment's crass press releases, where biographies consisting of out-and-out lies and fantasy are perfectly acceptable, have been co-opted by politicians. Famously, the racist British Prime Minister Boris Johnson was given his public platform initially by a BBC comedy programme 'Have I Got News For You' whilst Trump's rise was paved by his high-profile turn as the absurdist pumped tycoon in the heavily-corralled reality of 'The Apprentice'.

Pop buffoonery has a crucial edge on politics however. Where, for example, Keith Moon's destruction of his own drum kit was equally comic as it was disturbing, at least it had little bearing on anyone else. When Johnson leads an entire island to the self-destruction of an ill-devised, hard-right Brexit, for example, the consequences for the general public are dire.

RINGFENCE BUFFOONERY!*

* BUFFOONERY IN POP ENTERTAINMENT ONLY

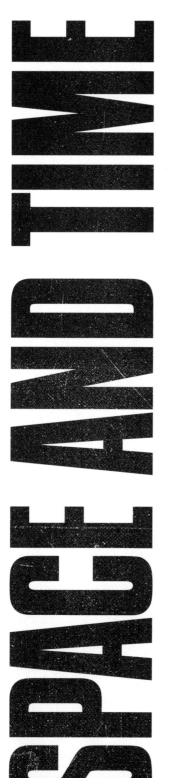

SPACE AND TIME

I played another show in London. It was a festival-type scenario so I deployed my signs heavily during my short afternoon set to help break the ice with an audience who didn't really know my material.

Richard Russell, who runs XL recordings, was also playing on the bill and watched my set. A few weeks later he was doing a tour playing with Bobby Womack for their album 'The Bravest Man In the Universe'.

11:01

‹ All Inboxes **Hey gruff it's richard...** ∧ ∨

From: Richard Russell

Date: 17 Medi 2012 am 17:38:54 GMT+1
To: Gruff Rhys
Subject: **Hey gruff it's richard russell**

I loved your signs
So much so that I would like to ask your permission to "borrow" the idea for some performances that Damon and I are doing with Bobby Womack this week.
We are rehearsing in NY today, and thought that Bobbys friend Arthur holding some signs with lyrics would be a nice touch.
Its directly inspired by your signs so I wanted to mention it to u and check if you were cool with it
Thanx for being inspiring either way!
Rx

He wrote to me asking if I'd mind if he used some similar cue cards during their tour. I replied, encouraging him to use them, adding that they had been a real break-through for me in terms of clear communication and that he really needn't ask, as it's hardly an original idea. Obviously, Bob Dylan deployed handwritten cards in his 'Don't Look Back' film over half a century ago.

In one of my life's highlights, Sally Grossman, who's on the album cover of Dylan's 'Bringing It All Back Home', once gave me a tin of maple syrup as a gift (we recorded at her studio). When I got home I poured the syrup on a pancake whilst listening to the Dylan album. As a fan I felt I was physically interacting with the album somehow. Was I taking hero worship too far? Surely it was foolish and ridiculous to think I could share space AND time with the icons of 1960s counterculture?

Bob Dylan
Bringing It All Back Home

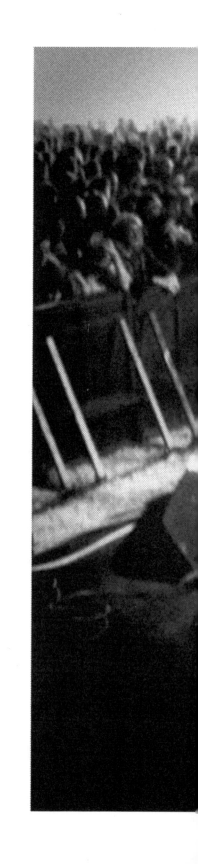

The festival in London I mentioned had been put together by the Africa Express organisation devoted to bringing African musical communities and ears into contact with those from other continents and vice versa, and largely associated with Damon Albarn's involvement as its roving musical director and champion. It featured short sets by a vast cast of musicians from all over the world creating a whole uninterrupted set that lasted from daylight, deep into the night. One of the unannounced special guests was Paul McCartney.

Incredibly, I was invited by the ever generous Albarn to accompany him on backing vocals as he knew I knew the lyrics off by heart to one of the songs he'd be performing: 'Coming Up' from the incredible McCartney II album, one of his best.

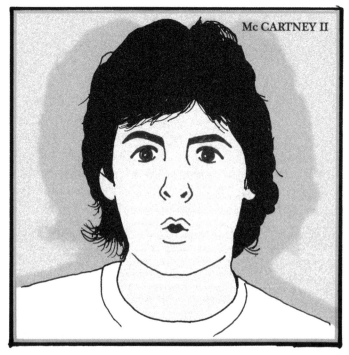

Artist's impression of 'McCartney II' sleeve

We rehearsed with him in the afternoon. McCartney played
bass, John Paul Jones from Led Zeppelin was on electric
mandolin, and Seye Adelekan on guitar. It sounded amazing
and Paul was a great band leader, patiently telling
all the musicians to simplify their parts. When chatting
to the French drummer he casually mentioned he had
flown in to London from Paris at lunchtime having been
awarded the French Légion d'Honneur that very morning
by President Hollande. An absurd tidbit to throw into a
rhythm section conversation at rehearsal yet undoubtedly
true. I was beyond excited, however, as now I was not only
sharing space with a Beatle, but actually sharing time.

I couldn't wait to play, but now I felt flu-like waves
of disorientation creeping over my aching body as the
impossibility of the situation seeped into me.

As we ventured to the stage and the song 'Coming up' kicked in, I realised that many of this comparatively young audience weren't familiar with Paul's solo oeuvre and deep cuts. Audience members were just standing around mildly reacting to that guy from the Beatles playing some jams that they'd never heard before.

In my opinion, regarding the song 'Coming Up', we are talking about one of the best-produced tracks of all time, and I demanded better for Paul, whom I'd only ever seen live in Beatles films surrounded by screaming hysteria and mayhem.

Psychologically, this was not Paul's crowd. It was just a physical group.

"I must get my 'cue cards'," I egocentrically thought to myself. I ran backstage and gathered up a medley of my signs, and I was back at my microphone before the next chorus,

"COMING UP!" I sang,

"LIKE A FLOWER ..."

Replied Paul sweetly.

Still the audience looked too miserable for my liking.

I began to deploy my signs, but with leadership of agents comes great responsibility. And as we know with bad leadership things can go wrong, leading in some cases to riot, civil war, unnecessary pandemic-related deaths, Disaster Capitalism, ecological catastrophe, genocide, pestilence, etc.

Back on stage, during the instrumental breakdown, I held aloft the APPLAUSE sign. The audience - around 3000 strong - began to applaud. I turned the sign around to reveal LOUDER. The open-air crowd duly responded. Songwriting genius Damon Albarn, my fellow backing singer, clapped enthusiastically by my side. As he had gotten me the gig and it was, psychologically, his audience, I thought I'd pass him the next sign to hold aloft. It felt like the right thing to do as I was so grateful.

"HOLD THIS UP," I telepathically suggested, passing him the 'APE-SHIT' sign, but before I could add, "whatever you do, don't turn it around as this is a London audience..."

Damon immediately flipped the board:

"TAX THE RICH"

declared the sign.

An earnestly-held view of his, that there should be greater redistribution of wealth, that is. So far, no problem. But still I felt a certain unease, as what Paul McCartney would make of it was a different matter.

I hadn't really hung out with him that much and I had no idea whether he still shared the opinions on taxation sung by George Harrison on their 1966 Beatles smash 'Taxman'.

Marvel at the photograph. McCartney is captured for a split second as he looks at the sign with bemusement.

But he's taking it all in and, I'm sure, formulating a measured, kind response whilst still holding down that killer bass line.

Empowered by Damon's onstage enthusiasm to the cause, the audience were, if not Coming Up, at least waking up and freaking out to the brilliance of McCartney's song, as they swayed and danced into the night.

The signs stayed on stage as hundreds of musicians including Amadou, Martina Topley-Bird, Charli XCX, Fatoumata Diawara, Baaba Maal and Spoek Mathambo rocked a near-continuous set. What a night!

More tellingly the London audience's enthusiasm for the Tax the Rich sign when it was presented to them with charismatic force by Damon Albarn is testament to the power of effective leadership. Maybe the London audience wasn't the problem. Maybe they just needed someone who understood them to hold the sign.

McCartney, meanwhile is a successful Pop survivor in a Rock'n' Roll paradigm, that, much like religion and revolutionary politics, is designed for martyrdom. Lennon's ideas are deemed forever pure, just like those of Aaliyah, Ché and Jesus. But what happens if you don't die or your band doesn't split up? A life (or possibly death) of collaboration awaits, ideas shared, ideals thoroughly tested whilst the romance, vigour, and rigour of youth falters. A band formed by wild musicians unable to hold down a life within the formal institutions of society becomes an institution in its own right. Leading any born rebel to instinctively seek to leave.

For the survivor, it's a slow burn to the inevitable end of course but, as the unlikely sage David Beckham once pointed out, it's never too late to redefine yourself or to tell your own story. But, perhaps, in order to move away from Beckham's kind of unattainable individualism, there's a case for pursuing Raymond Williams's idea of a multi-generational Long Revolution over a burn-out. For the cosmos over a singular star.

IBERIAN LYNX

My relative John Roberts from Trawsfynydd, Wales, was martyred in 1610 for being Catholic. He was hung and eventually quartered. Family tales claim that some of his friends carried his arm to Santiago De Compostela for burial. At least they got to see the sights and eat some Galician food. John's arm remains in Iberia. And his fingers were handed out to a few monasteries and churches here and there.

The Galician language has links, or — if you prefer — lynx, to both Portuguese and, more distantly, the Welsh language. In 2010, I released a collaborative album in English and Portuguese with Brazilian artist Tony da Gatorra called

THE TERROR OF COSMIC LONELINESS*

Tony's lyrics are profound and during our live shows the cue cards helped me translate some of his lyrics to a non-Portuguese-speaking audience. Tony became known for his music and inventions later in life and is an exemplar of a slow-burning artist.

[*The title was inspired by a Bertrand Russell passage]

WHAT CORRUPTS MY COUNTRY?

asks Tony

"VIOL

NCE!"

"HYPO

CRISY!„

"IMPU

NITY!"

"EGO

SM!"

"COW

RDS!"

"TRAI

ORS!"”

"CAPITA

LISTS!"

he explains.

He is a visionary in superhero outfits. I played a show with him in Sao Paulo in 2012. He unveiled a new anti-World Cup song (protesting against over-spending on ill-conceived projects leading up to the 2014 World Cup). The soccer-loving Brazilians thought he was crazy. But within a year hundreds of thousands of people were on the streets protesting for the same cause!

Playing overseas I started to realise that I could translate my cue cards into different languages. And to my amazement they wielded similar communicative powers in languages that I don't understand or speak:

DANKE

I was able to communicate all over the world

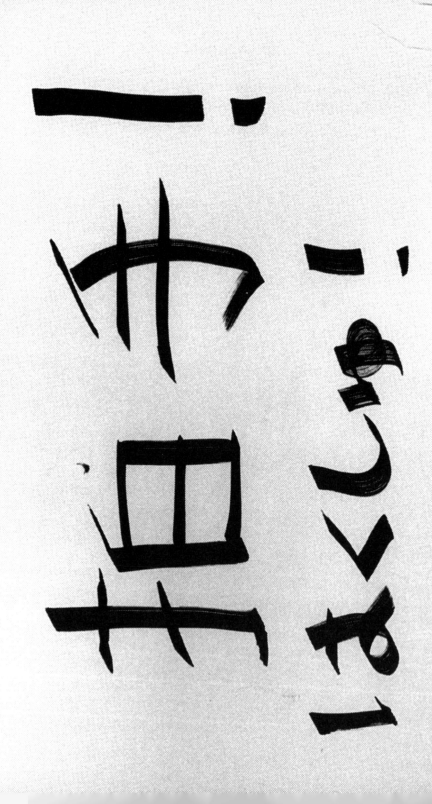

I added some nuance to my repertoire

PROLONGED APPLAUSE

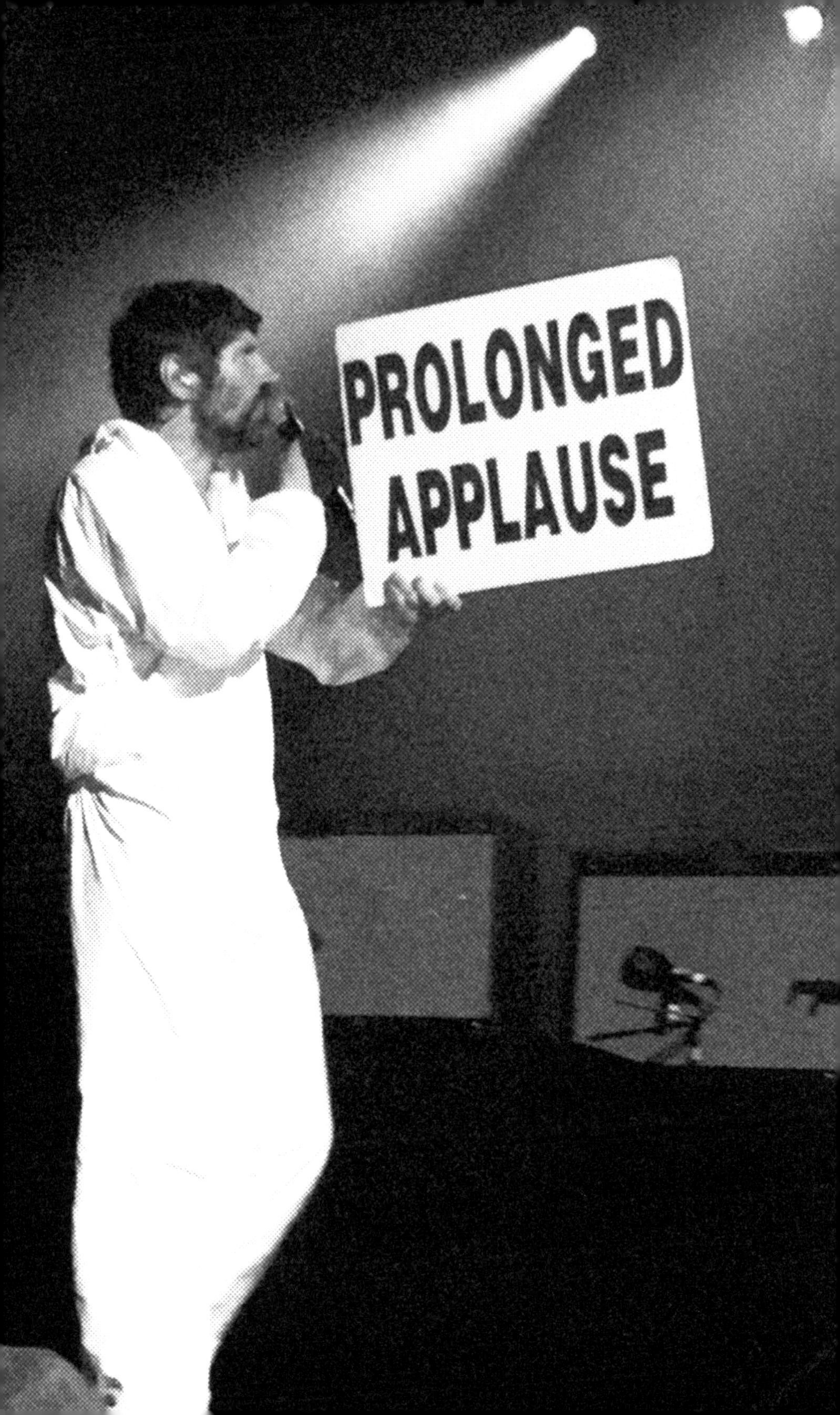
PROLONGED
APPLAUSE

A RIPPLE OF APPLAUSE

WYLFA
DIM D

SHIMA
OLCH

GENER
FESTIV
REACTI

WILD
ABAN

BURGE
FRANC
OPPOR

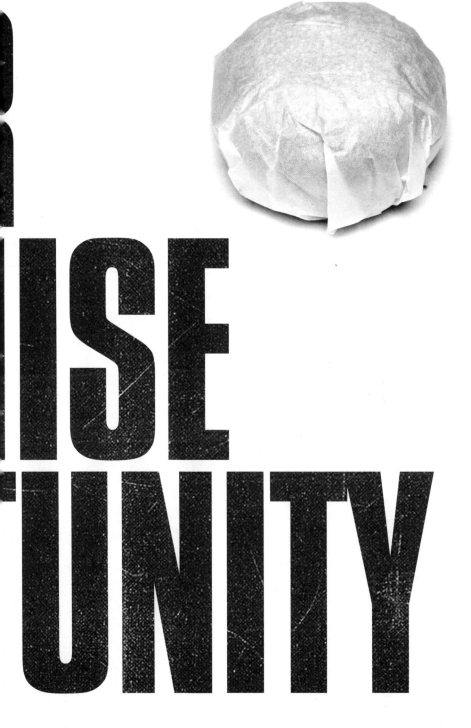

In the 2010s I was asked to conceive and perform shows
for National Theatre Wales — 'Praxis Makes Perfect' and
'Candylion' — and suddenly a whole team of technicians
were making signs and cue cards for the events. Gradually I
amassed hundreds of signs, slogans, and directives in many
languages. With the help of professional actors to hold up
placards, from the Berghain club in Berlin to warehouse

spaces in London and Cardiff, hundreds of people surrendered and followed these often ridiculous stage pronouncements.

It mostly went well, the only ethical dilemma occurring when my 'Property is Theft' placard was stolen at the Edinburgh Festival.

The next song is from 2018, 'No Profit In Pain' ...

THE MOMENT I WAS BORN, YOU PATC
UP TO STAY STRONG, DON'T RIP I
FOR SOME BASTARD BANK TO MAK
MONEY, RIPPING OUT YOUR HEAR
CIVILITY IS HELPING OUT, THEN CIVI
IS WHAT I'M ALL ABOUT. FORGET CAP
NOT ABOUT PROFITING ON PAIN. A
RICHARD BRANSON SEES DOLLAR B
KNOW IT'S TIME TO RUN FOR THE HI
OCIETY, WE'VE GOT   BACK A
EART ATTACK FROM C   LE TO GRA
E MOMENT I   U PA
P TO STAY STRO   P
R SOME BASTAR
ONEY, RIPPIN

E
T,
ME
IF
ON
'S
EN
OU
S A
UR
OM
ME
ART,
OME
FELT

ANNIVERSARY, YOU'RE THE HAN
STAIRS, THAT KEEPS ME ON MY
I'M NHS BORN AND NHS BRED
DIE LET ME BE NHS DEAD, LIFE'S
WALK, YOU DON'T WANT
SAFETY NET, FROM CRADLE
THE MOMENT I WAS BORN
UP TO STAY STRONG, DON
FOR SOME BASTARD BANK
MONEY, RIPPING
ANNIVERSARY,
THE STAIRS, THA
NO PROFIT IN PA

(BUT A SHOUT OUT TO ALL

There were graphic set-backs too. One of the signs that came in handy for crowd participation had the cartoon exclamation 'WHOA!' printed on it.

But signs would get lost, worn, or were too large to pack for foreign travel. I would get new versions made in various cities. Sometimes it would come back from the printers corrected to WOAH!

I was relaxed about it, much as I am with the style choices concerning phoney and phony, or is it phoeny?

WOAH!

Once however in Newhaven, Connecticut, my WHOA! ('Just print them out in your boldest font please') came back as WOHA! An entirely meaningless word.

I still deployed it in my set and it still got a cheer. People were happy to give themselves to the power of WOHA whatever that may be.

I feel WOHA, WOHA with me, We are WOHA, WOHA forever! The entire audience became one big WOHA absurdity.

WOHA!

It really drove it home to me that this was all about a sense of community. How we can find strength, warmth, reassurance, and Woha in each other. Even if a few dumb signs or an idiotic buffoon singer acts as a catalyst, music, people and community always bring the best out in us [even if you can't always sing in tune].

The crowd is wherever you find yourself at home, with your people; your Woha.

Which is why audiences gather in concerts and festivals and find much fulfilment and joy and a sense of well-being even when, say, witnessing challenging experimental performances, or camping in terrible weather conditions, that feeling of having lived through and been bonded by the collective experience of an exhilarating ORDEAL is what we search for in life, which is something that Stephen Reicher also mentioned to me on the phone.

He also studied one of the world's biggest festivals, the Magh Mela, where millions of Hindu pilgrims gather in Allahabad, Uttar Pradesh, India.

The conditions at these very cramped religious mega-gatherings at various holy sites in India should be extremely difficult in theory, but apart from an outbreak of cholera in 1891, and a few noted stampedes, the pilgrims in general leave reporting a greater sense of well-being and physical health.

I could apply this theory to the Glastonbury Festival.

Or even the theoretically underwhelming Dover Music Festival. Gathering with others has been scientifically proven to have huge psychological and outright physical benefits.

As Reicher points out:

THE CROWD EMPOWERS THE WEAK AND EFFECTS SOCIAL CHANGE

Which is why we shouldn't settle for less. As we face Autopandemia — the joint ages of automation and pandemic — and the workplace, as traditionally understood for many, breaks down or ceases to exist, we should seek a universal basic income for all and use our theoretically increased time for activism. For each other, for music, for the planet, for our descendants.

Evidently we won't always be able to convene in a physical sense at areas of human pilgrimage, whether musical, religious or political. In 2020, during a near world-wide physical lockdown, from Minnesota to Belarus and beyond, we nevertheless saw great agency and empowerment from the often distanced crowd to demand change. With ineffective Buffoon Leaders dominating a POPOBUIS World — we can still find agency as a collective. Just as the audience took control of the rogue van at Glastonbury irrespective of the act on stage. Because it's not about the author, it's not about the leader, it's not about the performer: they are merely avatars for the crowd.

YOU ARE THE AGENT FOR CHANGE!

RESIST MEANINGLESS PLATITUDES!

RESIST THE TYRANNY OF THE ARTIST OR BUFFOON LEADER!

DEMAND BETTER, AND ALWAYS

RESIST PHONY ENCORES

I'm part of an international
campaign called

RESIST
PHONY
ENCORES

We're administrated according to a cell structure and you're free to conceptually join us right now if you're in agreement with our four-page manifesto, check it out:

RESIST PHONY ENCORES RESIST PHONY ENCORES RESIST PHONY ENCORES RESIST PHONY ENCORES RESIST PHONY ENCORES RESIST PHO
RESIST PHONY ENCORES RESIST PHONY ENCORES RESIST PHONY ENCORES RESIST PHONY ENCORES RESIST PHONY ENCORES RESIST PHO
RESIST PHONY ENCORES RESIST PHONY ENCORES RESIST PHONY ENCORES RESIST PHONY ENCORES RESIST PHONY ENCORES RESIST PHO
RESIST PHONY ENCORES RESIST PHONY ENCORES RESIST PHONY ENCORES RESIST PHONY ENCORES RESIST PHONY ENCORES RESIST PHO
RESIST PHONY ENCORES RESIST PHONY ENCORES RESIST PHONY ENCORES RESIST PHONY ENCORES RESIST PHONY ENCORES RESIST PHO
RESIST PHONY ENCORES RESIST PHONY ENCORES RESIST PHONY ENCORES RESIST PHONY ENCORES RESIST PHONY ENCORES RESIST PHO
RESIST PHONY ENCORES RESIST PHONY ENCORES RESIST PHONY ENCORES RESIST PHONY ENCORES RESIST PHONY ENCORES RESIST PHO
RESIST PHONY ENCORES RESIST PHONY ENCORES RESIST PHONY ENCORES RESIST PHONY ENCORES RESIST PHONY ENCORES RESIST PHO
RESIST PHONY ENCORES RESIST PHONY ENCORES RESIST PHONY ENCORES RESIST PHONY ENCORES RESIST PHONY ENCORES RESIST PHO
RESIST PHONY ENCORES RESIST PHONY ENCORES RESIST PHONY ENCORES RESIST PHONY ENCORES RESIST PHONY ENCORES RESIST PHO
RESIST PHONY ENCORES RESIST PHONY ENCORES RESIST PHONY ENCORES RESIST PHONY ENCORES RESIST PHONY ENCORES RESIST PHO
RESIST PHONY ENCORES RESIST PHONY ENCORES RESIST PHONY ENCORES RESIST PHONY ENCORES RESIST PHONY ENCORES RESIST PHO
RESIST PHONY ENCORES RESIST PHONY ENCORES RESIST PHONY ENCORES RESIST PHONY ENCORES RESIST PHONY ENCORES RESIST PHO
RESIST PHONY ENCORES RESIST PHONY ENCORES RESIST PHONY ENCORES RESIST PHONY ENCORES RESIST PHONY ENCORES RESIST PHO
RESIST PHONY ENCORES RESIST PHONY ENCORES RESIST PHONY ENCORES RESIST PHONY ENCORES RESIST PHONY ENCORES RESIST PHO
RESIST PHONY ENCORES RESIST PHONY ENCORES RESIST PHONY ENCORES RESIST PHONY ENCORES RESIST PHONY ENCORES RESIST PHO
RESIST PHONY ENCORES RESIST PHONY ENCORES RESIST PHONY ENCORES RESIST PHONY ENCORES RESIST PHONY ENCORES RESIST PHO
RESIST PHONY ENCORES RESIST PHONY ENCORES RESIST PHONY ENCORES RESIST PHONY ENCORES RESIST PHONY ENCORES RESIST PHO
RESIST PHONY ENCORES RESIST PHONY ENCORES RESIST PHONY ENCORES RESIST PHONY ENCORES RESIST PHONY ENCORES RESIST PHO
RESIST PHONY ENCORES RESIST PHONY ENCORES RESIST PHONY ENCORES RESIST PHONY ENCORES RESIST PHONY ENCORES RESIST PHO
RESIST PHONY ENCORES RESIST PHONY ENCORES RESIST PHONY ENCORES RESIST PHONY ENCORES RESIST PHONY ENCORES RESIST PHO
RESIST PHONY ENCORES RESIST PHONY ENCORES RESIST PHONY ENCORES RESIST PHONY ENCORES RESIST PHONY ENCORES RESIST PHO
RESIST PHONY ENCORES RESIST PHONY ENCORES RESIST PHONY ENCORES RESIST PHONY ENCORES RESIST PHONY ENCORES RESIST PHO
RESIST PHONY ENCORES RESIST PHONY ENCORES RESIST PHONY ENCORES RESIST PHONY ENCORES RESIST PHONY ENCORES RESIST PHO
RESIST PHONY ENCORES RESIST PHONY ENCORES RESIST PHONY ENCORES RESIST PHONY ENCORES RESIST PHONY ENCORES RESIST PHO
RESIST PHONY ENCORES RESIST PHONY ENCORES RESIST PHONY ENCORES RESIST PHONY ENCORES RESIST PHONY ENCORES RESIST PHO
RESIST PHONY ENCORES RESIST PHONY ENCORES RESIST PHONY ENCORES RESIST PHONY ENCORES RESIST PHONY ENCORES RESIST PHO
RESIST PHONY ENCORES RESIST PHONY ENCORES RESIST PHONY ENCORES RESIST PHONY ENCORES RESIST PHONY ENCORES RESIST PHO
RESIST PHONY ENCORES RESIST PHONY ENCORES RESIST PHONY ENCORES RESIST PHONY ENCORES RESIST PHONY ENCORES RESIST PHO
RESIST PHONY ENCORES RESIST PHONY ENCORES RESIST PHONY ENCORES RESIST PHONY ENCORES RESIST PHONY ENCORES RESIST PHO
RESIST PHONY ENCORES RESIST PHONY ENCORES RESIST PHONY ENCORES RESIST PHONY ENCORES RESIST PHONY ENCORES RESIST PHO
RESIST PHONY ENCORES RESIST PHONY ENCORES RESIST PHONY ENCORES RESIST PHONY ENCORES RESIST PHONY ENCORES RESIST PHO
RESIST PHONY ENCORES RESIST PHONY ENCORES RESIST PHONY ENCORES RESIST PHONY ENCORES RESIST PHONY ENCORES RESIST PHO
RESIST PHONY ENCORES RESIST PHONY ENCORES RESIST PHONY ENCORES RESIST PHONY ENCORES RESIST PHONY ENCORES RESIST PHO
RESIST PHONY ENCORES RESIST PHONY ENCORES RESIST PHONY ENCORES RESIST PHONY ENCORES RESIST PHONY ENCORES RESIST PHO
RESIST PHONY ENCORES RESIST PHONY ENCORES RESIST PHONY ENCORES RESIST PHONY ENCORES RESIST PHONY ENCORES RESIST PHO
RESIST PHONY ENCORES RESIST PHONY ENCORES RESIST PHONY ENCORES RESIST PHONY ENCORES RESIST PHONY ENCORES RESIST PHO
RESIST PHONY ENCORES RESIST PHONY ENCORES RESIST PHONY ENCORES RESIST PHONY ENCORES RESIST PHONY ENCORES RESIST PHO
RESIST PHONY ENCORES RESIST PHONY ENCORES RESIST PHONY ENCORES RESIST PHONY ENCORES RESIST PHONY ENCORES RESIST PHO
RESIST PHONY ENCORES RESIST PHONY ENCORES RESIST PHONY ENCORES RESIST PHONY ENCORES RESIST PHONY ENCORES RESIST PHO
RESIST PHONY ENCORES RESIST PHONY ENCORES RESIST PHONY ENCORES RESIST PHONY ENCORES RESIST PHONY ENCORES RESIST PHO

Thank you to Mark James, Sheenagh James, Nemonie Craven Roderick, JC Gabel, Sybil Perez, Gareth Dobson, Mark Bowen and Chloe Walsh for making this book a reality.

This book clearly would not exist without my fellow band members and collaborators who I mention in the book. Especially so Huw Bunford who started making and holding these stage-signs with me with tape and pens around 2007 maybe, as part of the shared culture of Super Furry Animals. I didn't mention Bryan Hollon in the book but everyone in Neon Neon 2008 also helped develop these signs into printed cue cards.

This book started out as a weeklong run of PowerPoint presentations in Edinburgh and Hebden Bridge. Thank you to everyone involved directly or indirectly with those shows as otherwise this book most likely would not exist - including Nigel Klarfeld, Adele Slater, Alun Llwyd, Kevin Tame, Marcus Russell. All at The Trades Club, Hebden Bridge.

I engaged with Dr. Kiko for advice. Thank you Graham Erickson for more advice, writing and quotes. Thanks Pete Fowler for introducing Whoa! into SFA vocabulary.

The biggest thanks to everyone who sent in photos to the #resistphonyencores hashtag. And to everyone for coming to the shows. I can't thank you enough.

Massive thanks to Damon Albarn for taking me on some incredible musical adventures that seem beyond the realm of possibility.

Thanks Richard Russell for use of the email.
Thanks Paul McCartney for the unforgettable melodies.
Thanks to all the photographers involved in this book. Thanks to the Africa Express Organisation. Thanks NTW and their many actors, technicians and personnel for manufacturing and holding even more signs. Especially Wils Wilson and Tim Price for encouraging and expanding the repertoire of the signs and John McGrath, Kully Thiarai and Lisa McGuire for the encouragement.

Thank you to John Norton, Sioned Wiliam, Cathy Robinson, the Zoot family for helping arrange an unrelated radio show of the same name.

Everyone I've forgotten to thank - you know who you are - but do you really? I'm up against a deadline. Thanks in any case.

Thank you Flávia Durante for all your help.

Diolch Huw Evans am fenthyg copi o McCartney 2. Diolch Kliph Scurlock. Thanks Peter Gray. Diolch Y Niwl a Lisa Jên.

Thank you T on Tour, Lewie, Smash Corp and all the printers involved with these signs. Thanks Mark Foley for getting Festyval Wynd manufactured.

Diolch pennaf i fy nheulu oll am fod mor amyneddgar o agweddau anoddaf y cythraul canu. Ond hefyd am roi yr amser ac adnoddau i mi sgwennu a chanu. Yn arbennig Cat, MM, MM, MI. Mae arnai lyfr i Mabon Idris - un mwy teilwng na hwn efallai.

Mae Reu yn fyw!

Thank you to the taxpayers. You invested in my songwriting for many years as an unemployed songwriter. And I'm hoping I've been able to pay it all back and more. The main thing you need in order to create is time (and by extension - the resources) to do it. That's why I mention UBI as a way of democratising the arts and activism. The state will eventually be repaid and more, if it invests in its people.

Text © Gruff Rhys 2020
Design © Mark James 2020

Gruff Rhys hereby asserts his moral right to be
identified as the author of this work.

First North American Edition, 2020
Hat & Beard Press, Sierra Madre, California

ISBN: 978-1-7320561-1-4

Published by Hat & Beard Press
Sierra Madre, California
Visit us online at www.hatandbeard.com

Photo credits:
Alamy Stock: Shelley Duval, The Shining, The Beatles At Normal
College, Vonda Shepard, Iraq War, Political Leaders, Bobby Womack,
Bob Dylan 'Don't Look Back' still.

Getty Images: Mussolini's corpse, Boris on zip wire.

Adobe Stock: Drill, Hands In The Air, Lamb, Tumbleweed, Lynx.

Ffa Coffi Pawb — Rolant Dafis
Spacemen 3 — Craig Wagstaff
SFA Yetis — Richard Dawson
Cate Le Bon — Ivana Klickovic
Juana Molina — Marcelo Setton
Le Guess Who? — Erik Luyten
Africa Express Live No. 1 — Stephen Budd
Africa Express Live with signs — Alistair Burns
Cyrillic stage sign 1 — Joe Dunthorne
Cyrillic stage sign 2 — Max Avdeev
Drift Records / Sea Change

Candylion — National Theatre Wales
No Profit In Pain — Mark James
Drunk Girl — North News And Pictures Ltd
Glastonbury Festival — South West News Service Ltd

Stephen Reicher quotes from the following article: The New Psychology of
Leadership, co-authored by Stephen D. Reicher, Michael J. Platow, S. Alexander
Haslam on August 1, 2007
https://www.scientificamerican.com/article/the-new-psychology-of-leader-
ship-2007-08/

See also Drury, J. & Reicher, S. (1999). The intergroup dynamics of
collective empowerment: Substantiating the social identity model of crowd
behaviour. Group Processes and Intergroup Relations, 2, 1-22

Social media images courtesy of: Dylan Evans, Rebecca Rimmer, Steve Tamburello,
Jennifer Davey, Noriko Hirayama, Chloe Walsh, Stuart Curran, Llyr Pari,
Garret Keogh, Carys Eleri, Joe Lucca, Montserrat Balseiro

GRUFF RHYS has been releasing records, cassettes, and flexidiscs
since 1984 and is 20-something albums into a varied music career
as a solo artist and as a member of Super Furry Animals and Neon
Neon. He also co-created and performed in two immersive music-based
plays, 'Praxis Makes Perfect' and 'Candylion', both with National
Theatre Wales, and two feature films, 'American Interior' and
'Separado!' with ie ie productions. His first book, 'American
Interior', published by Penguin, was longlisted for The Guardian
First Book Award and shortlisted for The Gordon Burn Prize and The
Wales Book of the Year Prize, and also featured a groundbreaking app.

gruffrhys.com

MARK JAMES is a multidisciplinary graphic designer and artist
working across many creative platforms, including art direction,
video direction, photography, and illustration. His conceptual
work is inspired by a mix of popular culture and social
commentary and has gained a reputation for being challenging
and controversial. He has worked with Super Furry Animals and
Gruff Rhys for over 20 years, creating artwork, visuals, and
promo videos for the band and their various solo projects.

markjamesworks.com

OVERCOMMUNICATION
OVERCOMMUNICATION
OVERCOMMUNICATION
OVERCOMMUNICATION
OVERCOMMUNICATION
OVERCOMMUNICATION
OVERCOMMUNICATION
OVERCOMMUNICATION
OVERCOMMUNICATION
OVERCOMMUNICATION
OVERCOMMUNICATION